# POSITIVE
# LEADERSHIP

# Other Books by Mike Magee, MD

All Available Boats
The Book of Choices
The Best Medicine
The New Face of Aging
Positive Doctors in America

To Order: www.spencerbooks.com or 1-800-774-3313

Our order information number
has changed to **1-866-543-5140**

# POSITIVE LEADERSHIP

## A Moral Survival Manual for the Home and Office

# MIKE MAGEE, MD

Library of Congress Cataloging-in-Publication Data
Magee, Mike
Positive Leadership/Mike Magee, MD
148p. 19.2 x 14.2 cm.

1. Magee, Mike    2. Leadership    3. Interpersonal Relations
I. Title

BF 637.L4      1995      158.4

Manufactured in Canada
Third Edition

To Trish and our children,
Mike, Sue, Mitch, Marc and Meredith.

# CONTENTS

# Foreword

KAREN KATEN

Truly effective leadership requires more than a commitment to performance—it also requires a positive attitude and a healthy, balanced perspective on life. This is the power of Dr. Mike Magee's Positive Leadership. Transcending religions and philosophies, Mike has crafted a work of immutable, undeniable positive truths about life and how ones life ought to be lived.

While warmly told from the author's own experience, the actual voice is eerily familiar. It is nothing less than the reader's own inner voice, all too often lost in the din of our modern times. In other words, Mike's simple lessons are ones we know to be right and true, and have always known to be right and true—we may have just forgotten or misplaced them.

With its compelling clarity, Mike's work is more than just a useful reminder. It serves as a practical solution for those individuals and organizations that are experiencing a disconnect between their actions and their values.

Its timeless themes make Positive Leadership nothing less than a moral survival manual. No home or office should be without it.

KAREN KATEN

President
Pfizer Global Pharmaceuticals
Pfizer Inc

# Introduction

L
ife is lived as a series of conversations. We are instructed by stories, stories that extend and accumulate over a lifetime; stories that submerge and then reemerge, sometimes with purpose, other times seemingly out of the blue. These stories contain images as vivid and real as if drawn from the family photo album. They also contain deeply embedded values like individuality, teamwork, performance, innovation, integrity and respect for others and oneself.

These stories or lessons do not respect the boundaries of time or place. They travel with us as they instruct us, and attempt to make some sense of the differing environments we move in and out of each day—at home, at work, in the community. They beg for consistency and clarity, and attempt to bridge the gap between making a living and making a life.

They are presented here for three reasons. First, that in the telling, they may assist you in remembering and recalling your own conversations, some from long ago or as recent as yesterday. Second, that they might encourage your conscious recommitment each day to values that reinforce our better natures. And third, that in the listening and the retelling, they will assist you in embracing a positive approach toward leadership in all aspects of your life.

What you have before you is one person's stories, 10 cornerstone themes, and 52 personal challenges which are the distillation of values and lessons drawn from one life. They are no more valid than those of the reader.

MIKE MAGEE

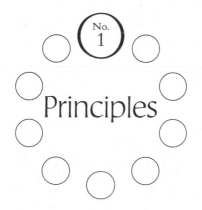

No.
1

# Principles

PRINCIPLES ARE AT the center of each human being. They are the architecture upon which our personality is draped. They are the cornerstones or foundation blocks that anchor our relationships with family, friends and coworkers. These principles are sometimes inborn, seemingly inherited as in "She has grandma's good nature," or learned qualities tested by crisis like courage. Principles are what speakers recount when eulogizing a lost friend. "He was kind to all, open and understanding," "She had values that she lived up to," "He was committed to a life of service." Simply stated, positive leaders stand for something, and that something has a visible impact on their worlds and those living in them.

# Be Nice

*"The meaning of good and bad, better and worse,*
*is simply helping or hurting."*

RALPH WALDO EMERSON

I t's remarkable how, in one's life, the most memorable acts of kindness are often simple actions exquisitely timed. There are many times when kindness seems to have been extended almost with divine providence, for kindness arrives when there is the greatest need, when humans are discouraged or distraught, when they are scared or hopeless, when they are about to lose faith in themselves. At those times, positive people seem to sense the need and instinctively respond. I grew up in a family of 12 children. I was number four, and by the time my wedding day arrived, everyone was used to the drill. But, of course, for me it was anything but routine. Yet on that special day, everyone seemed to be doing their own thing while I was nervous and overwhelmed. My sister, Pat, came up behind me and whispered, "Mike, can I make you breakfast on your wedding day?" A small gesture really. Yet, now 30 years later, I still remember how nice that felt and still feel a need to say thank you although I have mentioned it to her many times. That's the power of human kindness.

# Be Value-Driven

*"Assume a virtue, if you have it not."*

WILLIAM SHAKESPEARE

S ome leaders were blessed at birth with an active conscience, while others have been forced to cover the same ground as an ongoing intellectual exercise. Whether you inherited it or worked for it, an active knowledge of what's right or what's wrong is present in all positive leaders. And for this, they sometimes pay the price. When I was eight, a common pastime was hitching a ride on the back of cars after a snowstorm. My friends and I would wait at a stop sign for cars to stop. We'd slip out quickly, crouched low, and grab onto the bumper, with heels braced and toes up. Unknowingly, one day I hitched a ride on an unmarked police car. Now my father was well known as the town's family doctor. The policeman jumped out and asked me my name. "Tom O'Brien," I replied with ease, to which he quickly retorted, "Who do you think you're kidding, Magee?" Not blessed with a perfect conscience, that night my father explained that my lot in life would include learning virtue by instruction.

# Be Constructive

*"Any jackass can kick down a barn,*
*but it takes a good carpenter to build one."*

SAM RAYBURN

S o many of us view life as a matter of luck or good breaks, when, in fact, it's really just people helping people. Depending on the personalities, nearly any fix you find yourself in can end up constructive and instructive or just the opposite. I played third base for Rotary in the sixth grade. I had a great glove, a lot of interest, but still needed work on my skills. During one game a line drive caught me sleeping at third base and went whizzing by on my right. I tripped over my own feet and didn't have time to backhand it, so I knocked it down with my bare hand. My hand hurt for a week. I couldn't complete the play and felt like a real jerk. A month or so later, we had our annual Rotary awards dinner where the coach handed out trophies and said a few words about each kid. When he got to me he said, "Magee improved a lot this year. And he showed a lot of guts. Why, in one game he even knocked down a ball with his bare hand." I have always felt kind of lucky that that coach turned out to be constructive and not destructive.

# Be Tolerant

*"Everybody is ignorant, only on different subjects."*

WILL RODGERS

Tolerance is based on the firm understanding that perfection is a status all should pursue but none will fully attain. Tolerance comes more naturally to those who are curious and open to different points of view; to those who are generous and constantly reaching out; and to those who are humble and recognize their own limitations. My mother-in-law is such a person. As a mother of 10 children ages 6 months to 15 years, she lost her husband. Without insurance, without a job, without even a driver's license, she was left to fend for herself. Her unique ability to turn the tables was visible the day of her husband's funeral as she comforted the grief-stricken community that had turned out in force to comfort her. It's not surprising then that my wife would later exhibit some of these same qualities. On Mother's Day 1977, I had bought her a bicycle. We were into the fourth year of a five-year surgical residency. It was a beautiful day and our four-year-old, Mitchell, asked for a ride. Not thinking I put him on the back fender, had him hold tightly to my waist and headed down the road. About four blocks away, we met a gentle hill and gained speed. Suddenly the bike jammed to a stop as I felt Mitch being torn away from me. As I rushed to disentangle him and lift him up, I could see his sneakers and socks had been pulled off and his heels were bleeding. The crush marks were visible where his little feet had been caught in the back wheel. The strength drained out of me as my grief, my stupidity and my guilt overwhelmed me, leaving me so weak I could hardly lift his little body. As we rounded the corner, me in shock, he in pain, Trish could see something terrible had happened. Normally quick to speak, that day she remained calm and comforting. Mitch is 30 now, and if you look closely you can still see the scars on his heels. But emotionally, none of us were scarred that day because Trish reached out and reserved judgment.

# Serve Others

*"Life engenders life. Energy creates energy. It is by spending one's self that one becomes rich."*

SARAH BERNHARDT

My older brother, Bill, and I grew up side by side, sharing a bedroom throughout our lives. From early on I noted he was never alone. He was always surrounded by a widely diverse group of kids, all sizes and shapes, all backgrounds. People liked to be with him. In high school he began to date Kathy, whose energy, drive and determination balanced his strengths. From then on their lives remained intertwined as he sped through college, dental school, medical school and plastic surgery training, and she through nursing school and graduate school in social work. By the time he was ready to practice, they had three kids and he was prepared to launch what many predicted would be a stellar academic career. But in that first year, Bill and Kathy were invited to participate in a medical mission to the Philippines to operate on a cluster of children with severe cleft lips and palates. During the week, 150 children received life-changing surgery but to their astonishment 250 were left in waiting lines. On the plane ride home they vowed to return the next year to finish the job and did. But when the dust cleared, 250 were saved and 400 remained. More than that, they noticed that the caregivers who had participated were fundamentally and permanently changed for the better. It seemed the desire to help a child smile not only had a lasting effect on the child, but also on the family, the government officials, and the country itself. Now, 25 years later, I occasionally catch Bill and Kathy on television or in People magazine delivering the same simple message I heard after their very first trip, that changing one child's life can make all the difference in our world. Today their lives are nearly 100 percent committed to service through Operation Smile International, which has put a smile on more than 70,000 children's faces in 21 countries on six continents. Just as importantly, Operation Smile missions in the United States currently work with public school systems to identify children who have fallen through the cracks of the American health care system, children who would benefit from surgery and a new outlook on life. How did all this happen? Two people cared. Two people served. Life engenders life. Energy creates energy.

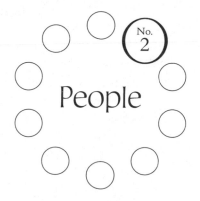

# People

EVERY POSITIVE LEADER I've ever known has been a "people person." The styles may differ. One may be an outrageous extrovert whose enthusiasm can scarcely be contained within her bodily limits. Another may be quiet and gentle, riding to work on a bicycle, and speaking always in the quietest of voices. But all have the unique ability to see the humanness in each individual, to personally connect one-on-one, to chip in and participate, to be content to be themselves and to uniquely tip the balance of life toward intimacy. When a people person enters the room, it feels better, happier and safer.

# Be Human

*"It is much more important to know what sort of a patient has a disease, than what sort of a disease a patient has."*

WILLIAM OSLER

B eing in touch to some means effectively communicating from a distance. But truly being in touch means using all of your gifts to transmit feeling as well as information. This emotional transfer creates dynamic energy between the two individuals that is real enough and valuable enough that sociologists now give it a term, social capital. In creating social capital, a gentle pat on the back is often more effective than a well-constructed letter. My father was a prime example. Sometimes I'd be standing in the office waiting to deliver a message from my mother or ask him a question and I'd just watch him in awe as he cared for his patients. His face, the ability to light it up, to twinkle the eyes, to wink and smile, the small laugh, the half hug, the full hug, the double handshake, the teasing tap on the arm or firm pat on the shoulder, the quick step to meet a person or rapid squat to get down on the level of a child and look at him eye-to-eye, the tear in his eye, the kiss on the cheek, the enduring hug. He had all the moves. He was human.

# Be Personal

*"Advice to a young man who wants to get ahead without any annoying delays: Don't write about Man, write about a man."*

E.B. WHITE

We humans are intrigued by real people with real lives. We are fascinated by hearing their names, their relations to the storyteller, how things turn out. We not only follow the story but also naturally draw broader lessons from it. In contrast, high-minded moralizations ungrounded in real events often lose our interest and fail to deliver the message. Successful organizations have the ability to tap into the deep and abiding need of all humans to connect on a personal level in the same way extended families have a way of extending their tentacles so that year after year new members are drawn in and new qualities are drawn out. Take for example, my sister Grace's husband's sister's husband, Jack Egan. I met him when we were both middle aged, old enough to have lived out some years, had successes and failures and become somewhat comfortable in our own skins. Jack grew up in a strict Catholic family with a patriarchal disciplinarian for a father.

Sweet, sensitive and caring, he entered the Catholic priesthood. His goal was to be a decent, passionate service-and-action-oriented man. From almost the beginning, he encountered irreconcilable differences between preaching one's religion and living one's religion. Through the tumultuous sixties and seventies he lived his religion, drawn to the most vulnerable elements of society. His notion of human service, of "breaking bread with others," of ministering to the flock, became increasingly concrete: real people, real communities, real needs. He eventually left the priesthood, though it's hard to reconstruct whether a rigid infrastructure of a centuries-old institution forced him out or the loving arms of people of like mind, body and spirit drew him in. In any case, it's fair to say that his transformation was a very personal journey, uniquely fashioned for him, and quite apart from the rules of the game. My wife first met Jack, not in person, but through his writing. We were at my sister's house on her birthday and she picked up a birthday card Jack had sent to Grace. She was so moved by the card that she said to Grace, "I want Jack to send me a birthday message like that." Some time later they met, and on Trish's 50th birthday a very personal note arrived from Jack which she treasured. We should never forget that our world is filled with Jack Egans.

# Participate

*"I don't believe in just ordering people to do things. You have to sort of grab an oar and row with them."*

HAROLD GENEEN

There's an old saying that if you want to get there fast, row slowly. It refers to crew teams whose competitiveness is as much a product of coordination, flow and equal participation as it is strength or skill. If everyone is participating and pulling their weight, and if they do it in a manner that doesn't compromise each other's stroke, their progress is swift and predictable. But if one sculler ventures out on her own, or another becomes weary, teamwork disappears and success is compromised. In 1960, we were parents plus ten and still all fit in one car, a three-seat Pontiac station wagon, four in each level. As soon as we'd hop in the car, my mother would start a group sing-along. For years I thought she had an overwhelming love of music. Later I realized it was a participatory, proactive and positive strategy to get us all "rowing in unison" so we wouldn't kill each other. It worked. The same principle holds true in the work environment where participation reflects well on the team leader. A fellow surgeon I knew made a practice of assisting the operating room staff in mopping the floors between cases. Not only did it send a signal to his team that keeping the cases on schedule was a high priority, but also made it clear that he was part of the team and willing to do whatever it took to ensure success.

# Be Yourself

*"Since you are like no other being ever created since the beginning of time, you are incomparable."*

BRENDA UELAND

People who try to be something they are not are on thin ice. You have to go with your strengths, whatever they are, and work on your weaknesses. It's impossible to do either if you are acting a role. Honesty begins with being honest with yourself. The quickest way to lose self-respect is to be someone you're not. It creates new problems without resolving the ones left behind. My youngest brother, Steve, received his college degree in Economics from Williams and an MBA in Finance from Berkeley. But he discovered on Wall Street that the pursuit of money left him unfulfilled. Today he is an ordained minister. After college my sister, Kathy, was a successful computer programmer with Prudential, but she found it too impersonal. She went back for her RN degree but found that too personal. So today she specializes in hospital information services. What many fail to realize is that we are constantly in the act of becoming, of using our imagination, creating a possibility, and then making it happen. The problem with living someone else's life is that your dream disappears and the good news never emerges.

# Be Balanced

*"When you have two pennies left, buy a loaf of bread with one and a lily with the other."*

Chinese Proverb

Simplicity and balance go hand in hand. The more complex our world becomes, the more likely we are to move off track. Those who are not distracted by money, possessions, fame and fortune, see with the greatest clarity. Proper reflection requires a sense of personal security and an absence of background noise. Time, not money, is the truest indicator of one's priorities and an excellent measure of life balance. When the kids were little, Trish and I got in the habit of awakening one hour before they did to quietly sip a cup of coffee, talk a little, but often simply sit in silence and see the sun rise and hear the birds sing. This was the only time when our world was relatively still, when distractions were minimal, when we could completely feel each other's presence. Now that the kids are grown and the original reason for early waking has disappeared, we continue the same pattern. It's become part of our life balance.

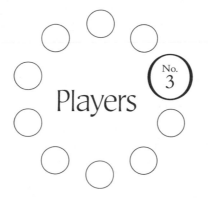

# Players No. 3

POSITIVE LEADERS RECOGNIZE that all organized societies, whether they be governments, businesses, schools, or families, possess both people and players. Players are those categories of individuals that tend to share common language, tools and approaches to problem solving. In hospitals, for example, doctors, nurses, administrators, trustees and patients are major players. In public schools there are students, teachers, administrators and school boards. In families there are parents, siblings, grandparents, in-laws and friends. An ability to recognize who the players are through careful observation, to understand their defining features and points of view through inclusion and communication and to develop sound working relationships with them by deflecting credit and extending compliments, is notable in all positive leaders.

# Be Observant

*"You can observe a lot just by watching."*

YOGI BERRA

To observe you must stand still and keep your mouth shut at the same time. I find doing each difficult, and doing both simultaneously nearly impossible. But with each passing year it becomes a little bit easier to quietly involve myself in the achievement of others without seizing the stage. Being in practice in a rural setting helped. My patients and their families always had little gifts and stories that went with them. They'd introduce me to their friends and families and a variety of interests, whether it be how to tie a fishing fly, how to gather wild mushrooms, how to make a guitar with your own hands or how to polish rocks and make them look like gems. Many times it seemed easier to listen to them and learn from them than from my own colleagues. My kids still tell the story of the time we were invited by one of my patients to go maple sugaring just after a rainstorm. We went up onto a big, tall mountain in Shelburne Falls, Massachusetts and climbed aboard a tractor as Bucky Dole headed off into the woods. You could see the trees with the cores dripping sap. As we rounded the first turn, I saw this white pail filled with clear fluid. Bucky looked at me and said, "Get that pail, Doc." I jumped off and obediently picked up the pail, dumped out its contents and threw the pail into the trailing cart attached to the tractor. Bucky gave me a dirty look and said, "Doc, what the heck are you doing? You just dumped a couple of days' worth of sap." The kids nearly fell off the tractor laughing, and I realized I needed to be more observant.

# Be Inclusive

*"Tell me and I'll forget; show me and I may not remember. Involve me and I'll understand."*

NATIVE AMERICAN SAYING

When someone lectures, we generally receive information with one sense. When we are shown, perhaps three senses. But when we are truly involved and fully engaged, we use all of our senses and sharing moves in both directions. I was once called to consult on a fellow who showed up paralyzed at the hospital. The evaluation uncovered widespread cancer of the prostate. The treatment was very effective and he had a miraculous recovery that lasted five years. During that time we became close friends. His name was Ernie Belanger and he was a retired engineer and metallurgist. He had an old farmhouse in rural Massachusetts and encouraged me to bring the kids up to visit him. One Saturday, I packed the boys up—ages 8, 6 and 4— and drove over to see him. He was in the back barn and ignored me but greeted the boys with great enthusiasm. He asked them to hunt up some small rocks on the grounds and bring them to him. They did and he carefully deposited them in a huge rock tumbler, which he started up with great fanfare like the master of ceremonies at a three-ring circus. He then asked if we could come back tomorrow afternoon for a surprise. By then he had the boys intrigued and they begged me to return. So on Sunday afternoon we reappeared and he excitedly ushered them into the barn. He turned off the tumbler and they peered inside. There were their pebbles now transformed into remarkable shiny gems. He then opened a little case with a key and inside was a variety of jewelry pieces from necklaces to keychains all awaiting a perfect stone. Each boy picked one and he fixed the stone in place. As we were walking to the car he said "You know boys, you're like those stones you brought to me, a little rough around the edges. But you keep tumbling around with each other— learning, growing—and pretty soon you'll come out smooth and perfect young men." About six months after that visit, Meredith was born, and one week after her birth we received another call from Ernie to come visit. He presented Meredith with a perfect little silver ring that fit her finger and a spoon he had fashioned himself with her name on it that has survived to this day. Many years ago Ernie included us. Many years later we are still including and being instructed by him.

# Deflect Credit

*"As for the best leaders, the people do not notice their existence. When the best leaders' work is done, the people say, 'we did it ourselves'."*

LAU TZU

Successful teams and organizations work through a great leader rather than for a great leader. This is because she so effectively communicates a vision, so wisely delegates and so inspirationally motivates that the team moves as one, all eyes and ears monitoring the creation and its impact as a finely tuned orchestra executing a composition in perfect harmony. A great deal has been written about leaders who deflect credit. You see examples everywhere —the boss who never forgets to credit her employees publicly, the conductor who turns away from the applause and summons the orchestra to rise, the engaged parent who, behind the scenes, selects playmates or teachers or activities to ensure success for her child. One thing these leaders all have in common that allows them to avoid the spotlight is self-confidence. One month before our wedding, in May of 1970, I was home on break from Medical School and visited Trish's elementary school. She had come up with an idea for a May Day celebration some months before. I remembered her telling me about it, how the different subjects and learning centers for her third grade could be integrated into the theme, how the parents would be included and how the children would be involved at every step. As March fell away and April appeared, the idea had clearly grown. Costumes emerged, a play was written and her home overflowed with construction paper cut-outs, streamers, scissors and glue. As the big day approached, her mother's dining table disappeared under a barrage of children's bonnets, strange costumes, Spring theme science and math posters and children's poems celebrating nature's rebirth. So I was well prepared that day, as I approached the school at 1:00 pm, to be impressed. But when I entered, the familiar hallways were gone and replaced by Spring tunnels with paper flowers and vines hanging down from the walls and ceilings. As I passed each classroom, one was more ornate then the next, and everyone was in costume—students, teachers, parents with all manner of Spring bonnets. It was clear Trish's idea had spread. The finale of the afternoon was a school play with a cast of thousands—not only flowers, but ants and caterpillars and bumble bees as well. At the end, the principal came to the stage and introduced the superintendent of schools who asked the day's leader to come forward to accept his congratulations. Looking for Trish, I saw her angle offstage and gently coax two young student teachers onstage to accept a standing ovation that I am certain they remember to this day.

# Communicate

*"Self-expression must pass into communication
for its fulfillment."*

PEARL BUCK

We commonly think we have communicated when we have not. Dysfunctional communication is a primitive collection of emotions, poorly organized, poorly displayed, variably reaching its target audience and failing to accomplish an emotional exchange. When there is real communication you will always be able to detect it because specific action invariably follows. This action may be more a function of how we say things than what we say. Great communicators will tell you that straightforward speech conceived in good common sense is important, but passion for your subject is essential. I heard a long time ago "Act in earnest and you will feel earnest." Communication involves the ability to inform, convince, persuade and entertain. It has little to do with dazzling individuals with exclusive knowledge, but rather with honesty and directness packaged in pictures and images that float before your eyes. Early in his life my brother, Jack, was a professional actor. He has a wonderful face, with dazzling eyes that spring to life on television. For my 40th birthday, Trish put together a video including messages from everyone. Jack had moved to California and I hadn't seen him in a long time. I still remember his "guest appearance." He was leaning casually against an old car, the camera zoomed in, and in the most direct and personal way, he wished me a happy birthday, acknowledged we hadn't seen as much of each other as we should have in the first 40 years, hesitated, and then said hopefully, "But maybe we will change that in the next 40." I've made a point of visiting Jack since then. If you are speaking about something that you've earned the right to talk about; if you are showing respect and affection for your audience; if you are appealing for action in a straightforward way with good common sense, then you will get a positive response.

# Be Complimentary

*"I can live for two months on a good compliment."*

MARK TWAIN

In many ways we humans are so simple. We are easily pleased by those we respect. What is positively amazing to me is that it requires little more on most occasions than a pat on the back or "you did a great job on that." A leader's job is to help formulate, motivate and congratulate. Recently I asked Trish what she thought of my eyebrows. She looked at me puzzled and responded, "Not much, why?" I mentioned to her that every morning before I headed off to school as a young boy, my mother would call me to her, lick her index finger and smooth my eyebrows and say, "You have such beautiful eyebrows." Now, clearly there was a part of me that realized that I was not particularly blessed with brows so unusual that they deserved this type of attention. Yet I still remember the drill. Why? Because this specific targeted transference of touch communicated that she valued me and that I was something special. She knew how to compliment, and it didn't take much.

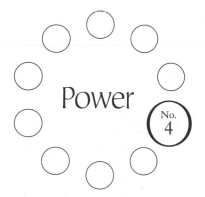

# Power

No.
4

POWER IS ALL about influence and what you do with that influence. The desire to define the agenda and move individuals to one point of view is universal. In fact, the dynamic tension that we commonly feel at home, at school or at work reflects our competitive instinct and desire to "carry the day." But what distinguishes the positive leader is as much the process of influence as it is the final outcome of influence; for she recognizes that the end does not justify the means, since that final outcome is a product of the means or method and the end itself. Positive leaders are alert to opportunities to advance important goals, but consistently exercise the high road in that pursuit. They are confident but never overconfident, and they scrupulously avoid reckless competition. In the exercise of power, the positive leader's rewards must be lasting rewards.

# Seize The High Road

*"I learned long ago not to wrestle with a pig. You get dirty, and besides the pig likes it."*

CYRUS CHING

To be a positive leader means to use power wisely and for the benefit of others. Power routinely corrupts, especially in the hands of negative leaders fueled by a predatory instinct and energized by the digestion of friends and foes alike which ensures a constantly shrinking constituency. In contrast, a positive leader's following is forever expanding. His power flows from example, an ability to unite and the capacity to convince and motivate toward the good. He views only opportunity in circumstances where most of us see danger and disaster. Take for example the great Cardinal Bernardin of Chicago who was stricken by terminal cancer. This followed by several years a uniquely personal and public challenge. The Cardinal was accused by a man, who had been assisted by a psychologist in seeking out "recovered memories," of having sexually abused him when he was a child. The man later retracted his story as bogus. A book by the Cardinal catalogued the entire event, its devastating personal toll on him, his public forgiveness of the young man, and their private reconciliation. When his cancer arose shortly after this trial by fire, many embittered supporters wondered whether the stress and wear and tear on his body had led to this. The Cardinal never made the connection. Rather, he focused on two things. The first was being a very public role model, embracing his death as his friend. The second was to share with caregivers what he had learned from his encounter with cancer. Shortly before he died, he addressed the nation's doctors at an annual meeting of the American Medical Association. As he looked out on the overflowing ballroom, he related to them that he understood their concerns with the rate of change in healthcare, their nervousness and anxiety, but reinforced society's expectation and the high road with this thought, "there are four words in the English language that have common English roots. They are heal, health, whole, and holy. I tell you this today to remind you that in our time, if you wish to heal, you must provide health. And if you are to provide health, you must keep the individual, the family, the community and society whole. And if you can do this, yours will be a truly holy pursuit."

# Be Aware

*"Don't think there are no crocodiles because the water is calm."*

MALAYAN PROVERB

Negativity is pervasive in our world. And negative leaders compete with positive leaders in every organization. In rapidly transforming industries, change adds fuel to the fires of fear, creating within the people a state of active receptivity to a negative message. Martin Luther King said, "The ultimate measure of a man is not where he stands in moments of comfort and convenience, but where he stands at times of challenge and controversy." But if positive leaders are to prevail, they must be vigilant. On the one hand they must create a vision for the future that guides and stabilizes transition, while on the other be prepared to challenge the negative messages of the day. I once received a call from a physician's wife on a Monday evening. I had worked closely with her husband, I as a surgeon, he as an anesthesiologist at a prior hospital. We had moved nine months earlier. She called to let me know that her husband was in trouble. He was a quiet, gentle man who was the anesthesiologist in whom I had had the greatest confidence. She explained to me that he had been tremendously overworked and had become irritable several times in the operating room. Two or three surgeons, whom I had known to be fairly predatory, approached the CEO and demanded aggressive action. His wife explained to me that a special meeting was planned for the following day to publicly censure him. She asked if I could help. That evening I called the institution's new CEO at his home. He had been on the job for only six months. He explained to me that he was feeling great pressure from these powerful surgeons, realized that this was a bit of an overreaction, but was anxious not to lose their support. I acknowledged the pressure he must be feeling, but asked him to consider the possible repercussions of his actions. If this wonderful physician who had served his institution and community so well for nearly 20 years was publicly humiliated, was he prepared to defend himself and his institution based on the facts if this normally meek and mild positive individual decided to confront his attackers in a formal, legal way? Had he considered the difficulties he might encounter in finding a replacement to serve in this small rural setting? Most importantly, what did he plan to do when the surgeons came back for their next victim? It might even be him. Confronted, a more moderate course emerged, and the meeting was canceled. The predators wanted my friend to be fired. What cured him was a two-week vacation.

# Avoid Reckless Competition

*"When elephants fight, it is the grass that suffers."*

AFRICAN SAYING

O pen conflict runs the risk of ending badly for the positive leader and the people she serves. Generally speaking, the negative leader is more familiar and skilled in the use of anger and confrontation as a tool. Negative passion often diverts attention away from critical issues and areas that demand change. Reckless competition emphasizes personalities over issues and drags everyone down. "Hi, Mom; hi, Dad. I quit the softball team today." That was Meredith's greeting one sunny evening in early June of her freshman year of high school. Through the years we had grown to know our daughter as an individual of great determination, not subject to peer pressure, who was remarkably comfortable in standing her ground. What initially appeared to be stubbornness in a young child unmasked itself by the age of five or six as self-confidence and principle-based decision making. Simply put, she knew what was right, and when she was right she didn't care what others thought. So when she came in that day, the starting shortstop on the freshman team at a school with a string of state championships, we settled back and listened to her story unfold. The coaches of the freshman and varsity teams were extraordinarily competitive. They had been very successful in developing talent and winning awards. In the beginning of the season, three freshmen had been elevated to the varsity. The freshman team had filled in the talent gaps, bound together and had been very successful. Now it was play-off time and the competition was stiff. A decision came down through the varsity coach to reinsert the three freshmen varsity players into the team line-up for the play-offs. It's fair to say that all the girls on the team—not just the three who would be bumped off the starting lineup—were upset. There was a great deal of talk about what should be done. But that afternoon, when their team took the field, all positions were filled—expect one: shortstop. Meredith had gone up to her coach, and in front of the varsity coach, protested the decision, letting him know how hard they had all worked, how they were a team, how this action for the sake of winning would compromise everything for which they had worked. When he reacted, "if that's how you feel, you can always resign," he had no way of knowing that Meredith would not hesitate that day to seal her own fate, and discard any future hope of local newspaper clippings, bureau trophies or a spotlight at the year-end sports banquet. He had no way of knowing she would turn around that day, and without a word or much regret, walk off the field. But that is exactly what she did. That team never survived the play-offs. In contrast, Meredith did. The following year, the team trainer, at Meredith's urging, developed a special curriculum for her in sports therapy. For the next three years, she was a familiar and trusted figure on the field and in the women's and men's locker rooms.

# Guard Against Overconfidence

*"A guest sees more in an hour, than a host in a year."*

POLISH PROVERB

I n the heat of a power struggle, it is easy to lose sight of your own limitations and ignore legitimate conflicting points of view. Winning becomes more important than understanding. Since you've convinced yourself you know all the answers, you become the source of both the question and the reply. I have become convinced over the years that most of us underestimate the good we do and overestimate our knowledge. The problem with the former is that it leads to discouragement. The problem with the latter is that it causes us to be close minded, to presume too much and to miss the signals. In so doing we eliminate hope. When I was a small boy, I would occasionally drive alone with my father who was a quiet man but loved to whistle. So he would start to whistle, and I'd respond, and he'd whistle louder, and all of a sudden we'd be whistling in harmony. Many years later when he was diagnosed with Alzheimer's disease, I accepted it as a fact of life. As it played out over the next eight years, and he literally disappeared in front of our eyes, I adjusted to this changing reality and learned to live with it. One Thursday evening I received a call from my brother, who was caring for my father in his home, to let me know he was rapidly declining and that I should visit. My father was 84. The next evening I arrived; and on Saturday morning I was sitting alone with him in the kitchen. By then he could not speak and kept his eyes closed at all times. But if you took a spoonful of food and moved it toward his mouth, he could somehow sense it was coming and would open his mouth to receive it. So I was there feeding him, having long ago accepted that he was gone, when, in a moment of boredom, I began to whistle. Immediately, as if by whiplash, his head jerked around, and his eyes, wide open, just 14 inches away, delivered the message, "my soul is still alive," reminding me that our limited understanding of the mysteries of life demands humility.

# Seek Lasting Rewards

*"It is better to deserve honors and not have them, than to have them and not deserve them."*

MARK TWAIN

Somewhere between choosing one's life work and doing it, many of us become diverted. We are subtly compromised by intellectual competition fueled at the earliest stages. Competition is addictive and not easily discarded. To win, to be the best, to hear our names stated publicly become the goals. The pace, the consuming responsibility, and the dampening of emotions crowd out normal feelings and challenge our commitment to family, friends and self. Financial rewards are offered to compensate for our inattention to our real responsibilities. Without a great deal of care, power does corrupt. Laboring for money, possessions and personal recognition are signs of a life out of balance. My path has carried me from the smallest organizations to the largest and back again, and the loss of potentially positive leaders to power, money, ego and fatigue has remained remarkably constant. We could all benefit from the advice of our elders. One study of 450 people who lived to be 100 outlined the following keys to their success: They kept busy. They went to bed early and got up early. They were free from worry and fear. They had serene minds and faith. They practiced moderation. They ate lightly and simply. They had a great deal of fun in their lives. Stated another way, "To be happy, have a clean soul, eyes that see romance in the common place, a child's heart, and spiritual simplicity."

# Partnerships

No. 5

POSITIVE LEADERS RECOGNIZE that no one is perfect, and that the whole is always greater than the sum of the parts. The individual styles of collaboration may vary greatly. Some embrace a prolonged process that allows every person her say even if it seemingly takes forever. Others' internal dynamics demand a more rapid pace and short circuit the system with multifaceted opinion-gathering techniques, a "touch-all-bases" instinct and a persona that engenders sufficient confidence to fill in the missing pieces. While styles may differ, the basis for partnership building is consistent. These individuals respect others and are careful listeners. Their ability to be a friend, while at the same time taking risks, instills confidence and loyalty and creates the palpable magnetism that consistently attracts new partners.

# Be Respectful

*"As I would not be a slave, so I would not be a master."*

ABRAHAM LINCOLN

Positive leaders seek not to control, but rather to inspire. The best are not walled off by steep interfaces and symbols of their own importance, but immersed instead in the culture and the people. Rules, regulations and titles arc not necessary to recognize these leaders. One need only follow the eyes of the employees and watch their faces, their attention and their comfort in the presence of their leader. Respect flows in two directions in a healthy, positive organization. As a young surgical resident at the University of North Carolina, I met Ruby within one month of my arrival. I had just scrubbed in for one of my first surgical cases. I was to assist the Chairman of Surgery on an appendectomy. As I backed through the door, hands up and freshly scrubbed, into the Operating Room, I was scooped up by a pair of arms and hustled right out. As it turns out, I had forgotten to put on a surgical cap, and with my hair blowing in the wind, Ruby had rescued me while the Chairman's back was still turned. Over the next five years, she guided and directed my progress in the operating room, along with hundreds of other residents. Short and stout, Ruby was a woman of genuine goodness, with a smile that went ear to ear and a personality that literally reached out and embraced you. She had been sharing her unique brand of leadership and friendship with young residents, taking them "under her wing" for more than four decades. Our love for her was simply a human response to her love for us. She taught us respect for the patients, respect for the surgical team, respect for the art and science of our work, respect for each other and respect for ourselves.

# Listen

*"Each person's life is lived as a series of conversations."*

DEBORAH TANNEN

Listening is an art. To some it comes naturally. To most, it must be practiced. When you dissect many conversations, what you find is an absence of listening, two people "telling" and "telling back" When I first began in management, I had a terrible time of it. Each week we would have a Vice Presidents' meeting and I just couldn't help myself. There was this inner voice that kept forcing out "words of wisdom." I knew it was obnoxious, but it was beyond my control. Then one week I discovered the solution to my problem. On my yellow pad, in huge letters, I wrote, "Shut Up! Shut Up! Shut Up!" I found I required this triple reinforcement. With time, it helped me gain control and learn to listen. Stay with the conversation. Listen rather than formulate your response to the next question. Time is a currency. The proper sharing of it communicates respect for another's contribution. Be mindful that your style may be too forceful or too abrupt, that it penetrates the quiet. In healthy organizations, quiet is not the absence of sound, but the presence of listening.

# Be A Risk Taker

*"There are risks and costs to a program of action.*
*But they are far less than the long range risks*
*and costs of comfortable inaction."*

JOHN F. KENNEDY

What is short term and what is long term is a function of the rate of change. At a gradual pace, it may be reasonable to concentrate predictively on circumstances five or 10 years out. But in rapidly accelerating environments, the best one might be able to do is to define actions six months or a year away. In both cases, the positive leader is thinking as far ahead as reality dictates is reasonable. She is predicting the fallout of short-term decisions, weighing, assessing and leveraging in favor of a long-term benefit. Successful risk takers are always attempting to limit the risk. They are grounded in reality and do their homework. Contrast this with one of our three young boys, who at age two was standing on top of a picnic table and without warning dove off head first toward the concrete. Younger and quicker than today, I was able to reach the pavement beneath him just before he did. He, too, was a risk taker, but he had an incomplete grip on reality and had no idea of the consequences of his actions. Positive leaders make mistakes. Some are large, obvious and embarrassing. But they never make the same mistake twice. And their capacity to learn, to evolve and to catapult off of a poor showing helps establish their mystique. They are human enough to try new things and willing to demonstrate vulnerability. But they have the uncanny ability to move from naive student to master teacher in a single step. Their willingness to risk failure simply reflects their knowledge that success will surely follow.

# Be A Friend

*"One may have a blazing hearth in one's soul,
and yet no one ever comes to sit by it."*

VINCENT VAN GOGH

A person can be the greatest thinker, the best innovator, the most stirring motivator. But if no one is listening then no one is sharing in it. Leading is about gathering—gathering ideas, gathering resources, gathering people. A positive leader is a friendly bridge; an individual skilled at moving in and out of situations and settings, in and out of organizations and communities, skilled at creating emotional exchanges that traverse obstacles and unite partners without long, word-intensive conversion ceremonies. Turk Newsome, a professor of surgery during my training, was truly a man of few words. I had perhaps five private conversations with him in my lifetime. Each lasted no more than 60 seconds. Each I remember. One was during my second year of residency. I was not on his service, but he stopped me while walking by on a patient floor and said, "Mike, remember, the difference between good and great is attention to detail," and then walked away, leaving me to ponder his timing of this message and its meaning for the next two decades. Another occurred at a 10-year reunion, when he greeted me in a crowded reception and said simply, "Most people don't understand what you're doing, but I do. Keep it up." Great leaders and true friends have ways of letting you know they are interested in you. They know what needs to be said, when to say it and how to say it.

# Be A Magnet

*"Make happy those who are near, and those*
*who are far will come."*

CHINESE PROVERB

One of the reasons positive leaders are successful is that their early investments blossom.
They invest heavily in esprit de corps, in the
creation of nurturing environments where all are valued for their contributions and ideas. These leaders
never seem to have a problem filling open positions
or recruiting new allies or friends. They always attract
a line of internal candidates anxious to join the team.
Positive leaders are magnetic. People enjoy being
around them because they feel better in their midst.
Spence Flo was a wonderful old surgeon I met when
I first entered practice. Everybody loved him, the
nurses, the doctors, the health managers and the
patients. I remember watching him and reflecting on
the secret of his popularity and success. He was a
down-to-earth fellow, relaxed and easygoing. He was
always telling interesting stories, stories filled with
real names and real places. He was known to say,
"Getting people to like you is merely the other side
of liking them." Within this realm he was comfort-

able and calm, never missing an opportunity to thank or congratulate someone. In his later years, he was somewhat crippled by an old neck injury and had difficulty bending low, and frequently asked his fellow doctors or nurses to help him with his shoes. He wasn't afraid to display his own vulnerability. He was a magnetic individual. Our helping him was part of his healing us.

# The Magee Family

The Magee Family in 1957 – all 11. (*Bottom row from left*) Kathy, Chris, Jack, Mary and Pat holding Sue. (*Back row from left*) Mike, Bill, Mom with Steven, Dad, Grace and Dan.

The Family in 1959. (*Bottom row from left*) Dan, Steven, Sue, Jack. (*Middle row from left*) Kathy, Dad, Mom, Chris. (*Top row from left*) Mike, Grace, Bill, Pat.

Mary, left, died in 1959.

Annbeth, right, was born in 1961.

Mike with Santa – 1950.

Mom and Dad's marriage – 1941.

Mike and Dan at
Confirmation about the same
time of Dan's motorized
paper route.

Mike in Rotary uniform.

Mom and Dad in the middle years.

In the kitchen, 1965
(*from left*) Jack, Mike, Dad,
Bill, Dan and Pat.

(*Clockwise from bottom*) Sue, Trish,
Steve, Mike and Annbeth – 1967.

Annbeth and Pat, the night
before our wedding – 1970.

Mike, Mitch and Marc
– 1978.

Our wedding – 1970.

Dad, Meredith and Mom
holding hands – 1986.

Oh Boy, Oh Boy, Oh Boy, A Girl!
(*Front row*) Mitch, Mike and
Marc. (*Back row*) Trish, Meredith
and Mike – 1986.

Christmas – 1988. (*From left*) Marc, Mitch, Mike, Meredith, Moe the Cat, Trish and Mike.

Trish and Meredith – 1987.

Mike and mother-in-law, June – 1991.

Oscar Elquero
with Marc.

Meredith gains a sister, Susanna.

Trish and Mike.

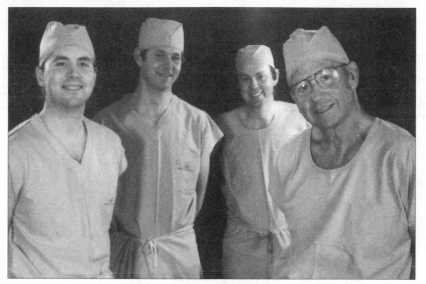

The Surgical Magees.
(*From left*) Chris, Bill, Mike and Dad – 1981.

Bill and Kathy Magee with child during an
Operation Smile International Mission – 1981.

Mike with his mother and mother-in-law.

Brothers: (*from left*) Jack, Chris, Mike and Dan. (*Missing from photo*) Bill and Steve.

Brothers-in-law: (*3 of 8 from left*) Don Ross, Sam Lewin and Rob Lattimer.

Sisters and sisters-in-law: (*clockwise from bottom*) Christine, Grace, Trish, Portia, Sue, Annbeth, Wendy and Kathy (*center*).

Mom and Mike.

Mom, Annbeth and daughter, Megan.

Dad and Dan.

A new life and the family celebrates.

# PROCESSES

No.
6

POSITIVE LEADERS KNOW that things don't just magically happen. Planned or spontaneous, every action is composed of a series of steps, whether it is the positive discipline of a child, care for a heart-attack victim or creation of an automobile. Knowing the facts and refining the steps improves the end product and the satisfaction level of all participants simultaneously. This is because most human processes were never thought out carefully to begin with, but resulted from reactive steps successively layered one upon another over many years. Whether inherited from our bosses, our teachers or our parents, these processes enjoy a level of confidence they do not deserve. Positive leaders critically examine how and why they do what they do, and continuously simplify, refine and improve. They are flexible not habitual, and embrace change rather than resist it.

# Embrace Change

*"If I had a formula for bypassing trouble I wouldn't pass it around. Trouble creates a capacity to handle it. Meet it as a friend for you'll see a lot of it and better be on speaking terms with it."*

OLIVER WENDELL HOLMES

I can remember as a youngster complaining to my father about a bad teacher and he would say, "Well, you better learn to deal with it because there will be lots of people you'll have to work with and lots of situations you'll have to deal with that you won't like." Sometimes trouble comes in the form of a negative person. More often, it comes in the form of change pushing at a rate that stretches our limits. This was never more clearly demonstrated to me than in the case of one high-school student who was a star skier. He was at the top of his game, possibly Olympic bound, when he was injured in a downhill accident that rendered him quadriplegic, with nearly no movement in his arms or legs. I met him nine months into his recovery when he was basically deciding whether to live or die. It was clear that what I was trying to do to help him was being compromised by a lack of cooperation and interest on his part. We reached a turning point one evening in his hospital room behind closed doors. I had a heart-to-heart discussion with him about whether he had decided to give in to fear and call it quits or whether he would choose to explore this new life and make something of himself. I watched his eyes as he struggled with his decision and with the momentous change in his life vision, and all at once you could see his competitive instinct and will overtake his fear and self-pity. It was an amazing awakening to witness. He embraced change and, with the support of his family and friends, he made a choice for life and evolved. By the time I left that community, he had not only graduated as valedictorian of his high-school class, but completed college, was on to graduate school and was happily married.

# Know The Facts

*"Don't ever take a fence down until you know
why it was put up."*

ROBERT FROST

There's an irresistible urge among young, aggressive and positive leaders to "fly by the seat of their pants." Since their instincts are generally good, they often get by for a period of time. But sooner or later the absence of good information catches up with them. Excellent leaders have the information before they need it. They have it because they ask the right questions, because they know where to find the information, because they surround themselves with people who know how to cleanse and condense it and because they know how to graphically display it in a format that carries the day. As a result, the positive, information–rich leader less frequently experiences failure and the need to retrace steps and correct errors. When I completed Medical School, I felt pretty well prepared for my residency. I was confident of my knowledge and industrious. There was only one problem. I didn't know what I didn't know. This became glaringly obvious at 6:00 a.m. on July 3, 1973, when on my first rotation, Neurosurgery, the Chief Resident asked me if the pre-operative blood work was all normal for the day's operative patients. "What blood work?" was my honest response. After the day's surgery was cancelled, the Chief sat me down and had a heart-to-heart talk with me. It was three rotations later and October before I had reestablished any credibility. Through the years I was reminded of that lesson. Once there was a brilliant surgeon who was tremendously "book smart" and could site all the latest references in the medical journals. Yet his judgment was faulty, causing him to operate when he shouldn't and not operate when he should. He did not know what he did not know, and was apparently incapable of learning in spite of the efforts of many. Another time there was an administrator who was very well schooled in the creation of complex statewide health campuses, and insisted on using the same approach in a more dynamic and evolving urban environment. He also did not know what he did not know, and ultimately failed. There's an old saying, "The older I get, the less I know." That simply reflects that openness to new ways of thinking and humility are essential for ongoing success.

# Simplify

*"Some of the papers presented at today's meeting tell us what we already know, but in a much more complicated way."*

Alphonse Raymond Dochez

The best leaders don't waste time. They have the unique ability to cut to the chase, and say it in a few well-chosen words. This simplicity enhances message clarity and demonstrates respect for others' time. The same direct communication styles have a way of carrying over to process design as well. Just as words are not wasted, neither are steps or time. Respect for simplicity and the real business at hand reinforces strong interpersonal relationships. In contrast, long-winded complexity distracts. But what about taking the time to just shoot the breeze, to show you're a regular person, to develop a relationship. The truth is you are usually interrupting someone's workflow. It only takes a second to smile or give a person a pat on the back. Do that instead. Our greatest success with simple, direct communication came on the birth of our fourth child, a daughter after three boys. While my wife was recovering, the neighbors helped construct a banner that we extended across the street. It read: "Oh Boy! Oh Boy! Oh Boy! A Girl!" It made the front page of the local newspaper.

# Be Flexible

*"If you look at life one way, there is always cause for alarm."*

ELIZABETH BOWEN

P ositive leaders move in and out of roles easily. This gives them the ability to not only offer help, but to actually be helpful. But choosing when to participate and when to patiently delegate can be tricky. The leader who tightly controls occupies his time with minutia and fails to create a positive expectation for delegation. He sends mixed messages to entrusted team members which interferes with the positive team bonding that naturally occurs when a team is entrusted with a difficult challenge. Sometimes being flexible means adjusting your style and needs to those of your team members. One of the great joys of living in New England during the '80s was growing up with the Celtics and Larry Bird. We'd all gather around the TV and marvel at what he and his teammates were able to do together. There were a thousand ways to win, and they seemed to be able to find the right one for each circumstance. It's scary to think what might have happened if Larry Bird and his teammates had worked for a micromanaging coach.

# Be Realistic

P ositive leaders are often guided by passion, passion for intellect, passion for work and passion for ideas. They agree with Yeats who said, "Education is not the filling of a pail, but the lighting of a fire." The same emotion that energizes them and fuels their success can also lead to their downfall. For positive leaders to sustain their contributions over a long period of time, they must reinforce basic values that cut across all elements of their lives, both professional and personal. They must invest time in revitalizing relationships, protect their families and frequently refocus their attention and limit their sphere of interest. This is especially difficult for the individual who is rising in her career because those around her will offer a wide variety of opportunities, all of which seem too good to pass up. For her, patience has not yet become a virtue. But burnout is a real risk and part of the reason why this brand of leader is heavily outnumbered by more traditional and negative ones. One good indicator of realism is proper pacing and proper negotiation of obstacles. As kids, we used to turn out all the lights and play hide-and-seek in the dark. We never had to set a time limit on the game because it always ended itself. Someone would start crying. We'd turn on the lights. The blood would be flowing from a collision. My mother would escort the wounded into the office, and my father would sew him or her up. The pace was too fast and the obstacles unrecognized. If we truly wish to protect the stock of positive leaders, we must teach them patience early and assist them in protecting themselves and their families by realistically planning and balancing their lives.

# Positioning

No. 7

THE MOST SUCCESSFUL positive leaders have an almost uncanny ability to be both creative and highly focused at the same time. They have learned to gradually shed "fuzzy thinking" at the edges and precisely visualize what they'd like to have happen. While others dream great dreams, these individuals follow through with immediate action. If not master implementers, they surround themselves at home, in the community and at work with doers. They are able to continuously evolve without losing focus on complex interwoven objectives. But they understand the secret—to aim high first, then focus. While soaring above, their feet are firmly fixed and perfectly positioned on the ground.

# Aim High And Focus

*"If you would hit the mark you must aim
a little above it. Every arrow that flies feels
the attraction of the earth."*

HENRY WADSWORTH LONGFELLOW

"Rigor and relevance." That was Marc's response when I asked him what advice he had received. He was exploring career options and I had arranged for him to meet an extraordinary leader to advise and guide him. "The point he was making, Dad, is that it's not enough to work hard and to focus on a goal if what you're trying to do doesn't make a difference or can't make a difference right now." As I listened, I thought to myself, "I could have used that advice a long time ago." It seems to me now that one of the crucial determinants in the development of leadership is the ability to focus on something that is both relevant and achievable. Hard work is indispensable, but hard work alone doesn't assure success. Success is about recognizing the unique needs of the present or future environment and matching up your interests skills and passion with those needs. My brother Chris was in Medical School when he first read about the early development of some new fiber-optic instruments that might allow doctors to see, with great clarity, hidden spaces in the human body. By the time he began his surgery training, medical engineers were just beginning to define experimentally the possible applications of this new technology. Several years after that, as Chris drew to the end of his orthopedic surgery residency, a surgeon from the Washington area traveled to Japan to learn one of those experimental techniques called Arthroscopy, and brought it back to the U.S. for the first time. Shortly thereafter, Chris became his fellow, then his partner. Rigor and relevance had ensured that he would have a bright future and make a lasting contribution.

# Take Action

*"It is common sense to take a method and try it.
If it fails, admit it frankly and try another,
but above all try something."*

FRANKLIN DELANO ROOSEVELT

I was raised on the adages: "If you think about it, do it" and "There's no time like the present." In general, the principle of immediate action has served me well. But it is worth considering my wife's grandfather's caution, "If you're considering a big purchase or a large decision, always wait two weeks before you decide." The expert leader is able to find a way to honor both these commitments. The first says that a reputation for consistent inaction or caution is inconsistent with leadership. Leaders are expected to have sufficient clarity of thought, spontaneous brainpower and inclination toward action to favor forward momentum. It is by action that the leader controls the agenda. But the leaders that stick around for a while can spot a landmark decision coming and turn the information-gathering machinery into high gear. You'll see them clear their calendars to attack complex problems so that the necessary delay to sort out the issues and make a critically correct decision is maximally contracted. That way their reputation for both action and enlightened leadership is sustained.

# Be Precise

*"The difference between the right word and the almost right word is the difference between lightning and lightning bug."*

MARK TWAIN

Effective communication is based on clarity of thinking. It's interesting how often an individual's confidence dissolves when he is asked to commit his thoughts to writing. For writing demands words and figures rather than thoughts and general notions. Some leaders resist the written word for fear of being "nailed down" on an issue. Others decline because they suffer a weakness present with surprising frequency, the inability to write well at a reasonable pace. They fear criticism, and as Christopher Hampton noted, "Asking a working writer what he thinks about critics is like asking a lamppost how it feels about dogs." Finally, there are those who stay away because they are not accustomed to collecting data, organizing their thoughts and making a succinct and convincing case. In contrast, successful leaders are able to commit their beliefs and arguments to writing, and are constantly bubbling to the top sequential facts arranged in a convincing manner. And those who are clear on paper are superior oral communicators as well.

# Be Evolutionary

*"Growth to man is a temporary surrender of security."*
GAIL SHEEHY

Nobody is perfect. We all have strengths and weaknesses. But positive leaders distinguish themselves by a willingness to wander into hostile or uncharted territory accepting the risk of failure and learning in the process. One of our very good friends grew up in a small town in Argentina. When Oscar was four, his parents sent him to school with their six-year-old son who was very shy. The village teacher immediately noticed the younger boy's interest and aptitude, and after that the family and the town got behind him. They eventually sent Oscar away to high school, to college and then to Medical School. One day he noticed a friend studying English and asked him what he was up to. The friend said he was studying for exams that would qualify him for a medical license in the United States. Oscar offered to help, working with him each night for a year and in the process picking up English. When the time for exams came, he decided to take them as well, passing the Science and English components while his friend fell short. Another friend was going to Buffalo, NY, for an internship and told Oscar of an opening. Off he went and was quickly embraced by his professors who felt he might have the makings of a surgeon and set him up with a training program in Philadelphia. Five years later, he moved with his wife to a small New England community and his practice grew. There was a large city 21 miles away with a sizeable Spanish-speaking population. Oscar reasoned he could be of service there so he applied for privileges at the large Medical Center in town and had his requests blocked by competitors for two years. Running out of legal reasons to prevent his entry, the doctors showed him a map and noted that he must live within 20 miles of the facility. "You're 21 miles away," he was told. Oscar promptly sold his house, moved one mile in and received his privileges. He opened a satellite office one-half day a week in the city and within one year made it his major site to respond to the explosive demand. For three years, the doctors who resisted his entry refused to say hello or even make eye contact with him in the hospital hallways. During that time, he was always careful to have a pen with him because he knew no one would loan him one. But they underestimated Oscar's lifelong ability to adapt and evolve. Within five years, Oscar added four more partners and had the largest practice in his specialty. He had gone with the flow, attracted strength and support along the way and faced challenges others dared not confront. Opportunity was there and he recognized it.

# Address The Real Issues

*"The mind of the bigot is like the pupil of the eye — the more light you pour upon it, the more it will contract."*

OLIVER WENDELL HOLMES

A common obstacle facing the positive leader is the hidden agenda. I can remember one time getting into a horrendous fight with one of my brothers who borrowed my baseball glove. My mother had to intervene and try to figure out why I was causing such a fuss. "Were you using it?" "No." "Did he hurt it?" "No." "Is it missing?" "No." "Then what's the problem?" What I wanted to say but didn't was, "Don't you understand, Mom, it's mine. And I don't want him putting his rotten hands anywhere near it." Whether it be prejudice, personality conflicts or job insecurities, hidden agendas are part of the currency of the negative leader who molds and kneads these behind-the-scenes issues, fanning the fires of fear to solidify his hold. Key to control is the process of segmentation, working multiple sets of issues in an individualized manner, hyperbolizing, suggesting, inflaming and preventing collaboration by instilling anger and contempt. Yet all cruelty springs from weakness, and combating these destructive behaviors is as easy as surfacing the knotty issues and exposing the need for constructive action. Doesn't the room blow up? Not in the hands of a positive leader. Her mastery of the language of human relations almost always allows enough wiggle room to present the issue and diffuse it simultaneously, sometimes in a single sentence. Once exposed to the truth, fear is no longer a weapon, and the real issues may then be addressed.

# Personality

### No. 8

POSITIVE LEADERS USE all their natural skills to connect. Their actions seem effortless, though non–leaders find these traits difficult to replicate. Their secret is that they love people and feed off the contact. To touch and embrace is not reaching out for them, but pulling in. They are pleasers and find their own happiness in others' smiles. They laugh easily. They are not Pollyannas, but courageous in surfacing difficult issues and combating collective fears which they do not fear themselves. They are personally secure, but not complacent. Rather, they are driven by passion for they believe strongly in many things. They freely expose their strengths and weaknesses. Their humanity is on full display.

# Laugh Often

*"He deserves paradise who makes his companions laugh."*

THE KORAN

Our first son was married by Father Eugene O'Brien, the priest who had married us and baptized him. In his sermon to Mike and Susanna he said that the most important ingredient to a successful marriage is laughter. He went on to say that laughter would cure 95 percent of the daily crises and challenges that they might encounter, and their strength, commitment and love for each other would surely carry them the other 5 percent of the way. Laughter does a great deal more for us than we give it credit. It introduces new people and ideas in a gentle way, but with exquisite penetrance. It exposes our human natures. It places our human flaws and environmental problems on the table where they can be addressed. It breaks the tension when things are getting too hot and livens the mood when emotions are too cold. Humor reflects intelligence and quickness. It is the shortest distance between two people. Humor for a positive leader involves real and personal stories that expose humanity and vulnerability. My sister, Sue, was number 10 in the family. As she emerged from adolescence, my mother had had just about enough with the surliness of the teenage years. Sue had a habit of coming in from high school each day with a frown on her face, and without so much as a hello to my mother, would bark, "What's for dinner?" One day, to her surprise, my mother shot back, "Fried shit, Susie, that's what we're having. Fried shit!" They both laughed and her behavior improved.

# Touch And Embrace

*"The biggest disease today is not leprosy or tuberculosis, but rather the feeling of being unwanted."*

MOTHER THERESA

Health care is one of the few professional areas where human touch is an expectation, rather than an invasion of privacy. In most fields of work, an individual's space is rigidly adhered to. Yet in the health professions, lack of touch is considered a failing. This reflects all humans' need for intimacy, especially when emotionally or physically compromised, as well as the real role that touch plays in healing. When I first began in practice, I was surprised how my patients cared for me. Many of them were older and I must have seemed quite young and needy. They'd pat me on the back when they came to see me, or rub the side of my arm, or grab my hand and insert it into the hand of their husband or wife, "This is my doctor." They'd have me hold their grandchildren and do hundreds of other little things that conspired to put me in physical contact with themselves and their lives. They seemed to understand that I needed that. I would, in turn, extend myself physically their way, and I began to notice and catalog over the years the best examples. I once had a patient dying of cancer who was bedridden in the hospital and preparing for death. I came around on rounds one morning and discovered, to my surprise, the patient dancing with a nurse in his room. He was beaming. The nurse noted my disbelief and said to me, "He wanted to dance one more time." What a wonderful person she was. What a wonderful leader she was.

# Overcome Fear

*"It is not power that corrupts, but fear. The fear of losing power corrupts those who wield it, and the fear of the scourge of power corrupts those who are subject to it."*

AUNG SAN SUU KYI

N egative leaders have great power in our world and in our daily lives because fear is a powerful currency. Fear is easy to exchange and easy to access. It can be counted on in most environments to draw an immediate response. The negative leader, when challenged about his methods, will frequently respond, "I'm just being brutally honest." Yet, as one man has said, these individuals "get more satisfaction from the brutality than from the honesty." Those who cower in fear also bear responsibility. They have not defined what will be the ethical limit for them. How far will they be pushed before resisting? The job of positive leadership involves not only confronting the source of fear, but also liberating its subjects. I once discussed this issue with a colleague, a bright, outgoing individual who had grown up poor but with strong ethical roots. Along the way, in the pursuit of power and other rewards, he had developed allegiances with individuals less grounded.

When I challenged him on what he was becoming, he responded that he was already in too deep, owed too much and had promised loyalty. He said, "The same will happen to you." I wondered if that was true, but then realized that there was nothing that he had that I wanted. I had already defined my ethical limits. And within those parameters, I was protected from his influence. As Eleanor Roosevelt noted, "No one can make you feel inferior without your consent."

---

# Lead In Crisis

*"In Chinese, the word for crisis is weiji, composed of the character wei, which means danger, and ji, which means opportunity."*

JAN WONG

At various stages in my career I have been immersed in crisis. Some have been very personal like being a 25-year-old resident caring for a two- and three-year-old brother and sister, each with 90 percent burns, each of whom eventually died. Other times I have entered voluntarily because the situation required some positive intervention. There was the death of a 35-year-old head nurse who was everybody's favorite in a small rural hospital. She was suddenly lost to a brain aneurysm. I wrote an editorial in our local newspaper the next morning. Another time we lost a wonderful and gentle surgeon to an automobile accident. He was 52 and had married late in life. He had two young boys. I assisted behind-the-scenes in the memorial arrangements. These were small gestures, but properly timed. If there is ever a need to exercise positive leadership, it is at times of crisis and tragedy; for these moments of struggle invite the participation of people who can see beyond the event and who instinctively sense the lesson to be learned—people who can take the powerful and potentially destructive emotions that have escaped and channel them to some constructive good.

# Be Passionate

A long time ago, Dale Carnegie wrote *The Quick and Easy Way to Effective Speaking*. In it he mentioned that he had never witnessed a poor speech if the speaker presented material about which he had both knowledge and passion. Those who believe, and believe strongly, present their cases in real-life terms and with a sense of urgency transmitted in voice, gesture, eye contact and facial expression. When Michael was a sophomore at Deerfield Academy in Massachusetts he became entangled in a controversy. There was a half-century-old event called "The Sophomore Declamation Contest." It was a way of promoting public speaking skills in tenth graders. The idea was this: every kid in every English class had to prepare a piece for public presentation. The recitations could be any length. Each class would then choose three of their classmates based on their overall presentation skills to move on to the next step in the contest. When it came to Michael, he choose a three-sentence recitation just to get it over with. His teacher refused to let him get away with that and sent him back to the drawing board with the instruction, "Bring me something that excites you." When his turn came up a few days later, he stood and recited the entire Arlo Guthrie rendition of "Alice's Restaurant" with such passion and conviction that he received a standing ovation. The piece was 17 minutes long. He went on to perform it again in the class-wide competition and survived once again, with nine others destined for the finals. The finals were to be held as part of Alumni Weekend. Several days before the event, the Chairman of the English department told him the piece was too long and that he'd need to edit it down. Michael explained to him that it couldn't be done because after all, this was a saga, a continuous tale about Arlo's confrontation with a Massachusetts local police chief, and to interrupt the chain of events would destroy the story. Still, the department Chairman insisted. But by then Michael was Arlo, and said if that were the case, he simply would have to withdraw. Of course, we knew nothing of this. We dragged the whole family to the weekend of events and followed the instructions, which included attending the finals of Sophomore Declamation at 2:00 p.m. in Alumni Hall. The place was packed and we picked up a program. To our surprise, there was Michael's name listed among the presenters. All the others had recognized classics from English literature listed opposite their names. So when Trish and I read "Alice's Restaurant" next to Mike's, we just looked at each other. Next thing we knew, there were ten kids sitting up on the stage, all of them dressed in required slacks, blazers and ties, except one. Michael had the tie (hanging down loose), but instead of slacks he had torn and patched blue jeans and instead of the blazer, there was a jean jacket and a bandanna around his head. The presentations began, one by one, none beyond seven minutes, and all remarkably well done. Number nine was a tall handsome blonde-haired boy. He had a deep radio voice, and with a full British accent, delivered Gunga Din flawlessly. As the applause was subsiding, Michael pulled his chair slovenly to center stage, and slumped himself down with a look of disgust at the audience, and began to tell his story. And halfway through, I swear the audience knew in their hearts that Arlo was among them. And they laughed and cried; they really did. So as not to brag, I won't tell you who won that day, but I will tell you this. He was a youth of great passion. And he held the audience in his hands for a full 17 minutes.

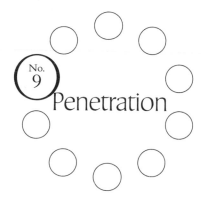

# Penetration

No.
9

WHEN POSITIVE LEADERS make a point, people listen and remember. These leaders possess exquisite timing, persistence and the unique ability to seize the moment. They are courageous, often opposing a majority point of view, but never without some certainty of a successful outcome. They pick their battles wisely and only when they believe that a significant issue is at stake. At those times, they hold on as tightly to an issue as a dog on a pants leg. This determination, combined with an aura of "being right most of the time," is a large part of their success. But their real ability to penetrate the mind and spirit lies in their verbal skill of painting vivid pictures that graphically display the potential good and bad outcomes of the decisions at hand. When their listeners "see it," they usually see it their way.

# Be Courageous

*"One man with courage is a majority."*

ANDREW JACKSON

N egative leaders have a distinct advantage over positive ones in our world. Their currency— anger, unbridled passion and fear—is easily acquired. The emotion of hatred is forward moving and target specific. But perhaps most important is the fact that negative leadership works. It draws a rapid response from the audience. This is because the majority of our external and internal conversations—reflected in gossip, in what we engage in through media and in what we think and worry about—is negatively based. To confront this environment, the positive leader must courageously attack on two fronts. First, she must publicly, confidently and calmly confront the negative leader. Secondly, she must commit to educating and inspiring her followers, to emptying their minds of the negative and to filling their minds with concrete goals and a future that are attainable. The positive leader uses role modeling and exquisite timing for this two-prong attack. Take, for example, the action of Rosa Parks in refusing to go to the back of the bus in Montgomery,

Alabama. Simultaneously, this quiet act of courage from a most unlikely source confronted an evil and, to that point, impenetrable empire while at the same time galvanizing the American people to pursue a more hopeful future. A simple act of courage. That's all it was. A single act of courage by a woman who instinctively knew what President Clinton would put in words some 30 years later – that "There is nothing wrong with America that cannot be cured by what is right with America."

# Be Different

*"There is nothing noble about being superior to some other man. The true nobility is in being superior to your previous self."*

HINDU PROVERB

When you grow up in a large family, you appreciate early the value of being different. Much of what life's about is an inner struggle to define and become comfortable with who you uniquely are. That must be done while at the same time learning to appreciate the uniqueness and style of the varied personalities that you meet and interact with each day. If I have been aided by growing up in the presence of 11 brothers and sisters and 10 members of my wife's family, our children have been doubly blessed. At their birth, they had 40 aunts and uncles, 20 from our direct families, paired with 20 others from a vast array of family experiences, cultures and backgrounds. Each of these is different, one from another. But beyond that are their extended families, several of which provide unique examples of personal evolution and the progressive stepwise discovery of new ways of being different in a single life. My oldest sister, Grace, is married to Sam

Lewin. His mother, Jeanette, is a perfect example of continuous ongoing differentiation. She grew up in Jersey City, New Jersey and after college became a registered nurse. Her first love was emergency room and operating room nursing. Within a short time she was married and together with her husband, a pharmacist, opened a local drug store. As the business grew, they also raised two children and she became an expert in purchasing and sales. Off of that platform, she became aggressively involved in community activities and volunteerism, becoming the President of the DeBoer Heart Hospital Volunteer Support Group and the President of Hadassah. As those challenges were met, she marched forward and went back to school receiving a Bachelors and Masters in nursing. At age 50, she launched a new career becoming a school nurse and subsequently an administrator of school nursing for the Jersey City school system. After 25 years, at age 75, she retired and immediately transitioned into an active role with the Meals on Wheels organization. When my wife recently expressed amazement at her level of engagement, she responded, "What else am I going to do with my time? I like to help people." Being different means more than defining your uniqueness compared to others in this world; it also means constantly evolving and being different from your former self.

# Seize The Moment

*"Only those who dare to fail greatly
can ever achieve greatly."*

ROBERT F. KENNEDY

P ositive leaders seem to have the most exquisite timing. Yet often when you scratch beneath the surface, what appears to have been spontaneous was well planned. It is their excellent preparation that frees up positive leaders to recognize opportunities at hand and act on them with apparent ease. My brother, Danny, has always been like that. One day my father received a call from a little old lady who lived several blocks away. She was calling him to say how proud he must be to have a son like Danny, so helpful and courteous. My father thanked her and inquired what event had led to her call. She said, "Oh, your son picked me up in his car at 6:30 this morning as I walked in the rain to church." Now, I'm sure my father would have appreciated Danny's good will gesture had it not been for the fact that he was eleven. It turns out that Danny had a lucrative paper route, now up to 100 papers a day, which he managed to deliver "on time, all the time" by using the family car. Propped up on two folded pillows, Danny had been about his appointed motorized rounds for the past six months, and along the way had been "seizing the moment" whenever an opportunity arose. The day he lost his wheels, he did not mourn. He had already established his reputation as a dramatic and decidedly positive leader. And he remains one to this day.

# Be A Visionary

*"New opinions are always suspected, and usually
are opposed without any other reason but because
they are not already common."*

JOHN LOCKE

A s a product of Jesuit schools, I was taught that
mediocrity was the greatest sin. What I have
learned since then is that the opportunity to
reach your full potential is most clearly affected by
the extent of your vision. This is as true for the evolving leader as it is for the newborn. At Pennsylvania
Hospital in Philadelphia Trish set up the "Ready to
Learn Center" in the Women and Infants Clinic. Its
mission was to promote learning from the first day of
life for at-risk parents and children. It included a
model play center, advice on quality pre-school
activities, promotion of neighborhood learning and
enhancement of intergenerational relationships that
would empower parents with the skills to provide an
enriched and secure environment for their children.
The training of parents as teachers began before the
babies were even born. And the early childhood edu-
cators spent as much time training those on the
health delivery team as they did the parents and chil-

dren. The concept was new, that educational poten
tial tied directly to one's health. But the extra focus
paid off in a more positive environment and a broader vision of what health is all about. Simultaneously
others were making the same discovery. And today, in
many sites around the country, pediatricians provide
parents with books for their children as part of the
well-baby visit through a national program called
"Reach Out and Read." To succeed at anything you
have to be able to envision the goal and focus all of
your energy and training upon it. And for every great
leader out there, there were one or two mentors who
recognized that individual's potential early, adjusted it
upward, and intervened to encourage and sustain the
leader along the way to her appointed mission.

# Be Persistent

*"What does not destroy me makes me stronger."*

FREDERICK NIETZSCHE

P ersistence requires equal measures of strength and determination. How far you push and how long you persist is a matter of judgment. When I was 17, I received my driver's permit. I desperately wanted to drive. My oldest sister, Grace, was coming home from college on a semester break and was being dropped off at her friend's house 30 miles away. I asked my mother if I could go with her and if I could drive. She said yes. At first everything went well. We made it out of the garage and driveway. I was steady on the highway. The turn off was fine and I responded to her directions appropriately. As we made the final right onto Maple Street, she pointed to the target driveway. Signal on, I relaxed and that's when it happened. Somehow as my foot went for the brake, it hit the gas, which would not have been so bad if an antique T-Bird hadn't been in the driveway, which would not have been so bad if the garage door had been open and the T-Bird hadn't gone through it, which would not have been so bad if there hadn't been a brand new Cadillac inside the garage. When the dust settled, both cars and the garage were in shambles. After my sister got into the car, I asked my mother if I could drive home. I was surprised at my mother's response as she looked at me. "Are you crazy?" "What's the matter, Mom, don't you trust me?" I inquired.

# Positivity

POSITIVE LEADERS ARE used to being initially underestimated; for on the surface, they may appear different, out of touch and vulnerable. But beneath, they are focused and resilient, capable of laboring against great odds with little reinforcement. Their strength is a reflection of their unerring faith in a greater good. Their secret is that they find good in all, and are able to consistently forgive and seek forgiveness. They disarm and convert by their example. Their dreams expand to include the dreams of others. Their seemingly limitless energy streams in from those who love them and commit to regularly revitalizing them. But their lasting trait is a deeply seated confidence in themselves, for positive leaders like who they are.

# Have Faith

*"Although the world is full of suffering,*
*it is also full of overcoming it."*

HELEN KELLER

The most difficult portion of my training in surgery came during my second year of residency
when I was on the pediatric heart team. My
job was to take care of the babies in the Intensive
Care Unit after surgery, to keep them alive. One
Thursday night a very sick child, barely alive, arrived
after surgery. The child had been born with an
abnormal heart and the mother had refused care. As
the child came closer to death, state troopers had
been sent out to bring the child in. That first night
after surgery, the child died, too far gone to be saved.
I was instructed to notify the mother. I called her, and
as best and as gently as I could, told her that her baby
had died. But as soon as I uttered the words, I heard
her drop the phone and run, her screams waxing and
waning as she ran from room to room. I was crushed.
After a few hours sleep, and a full day of work, I set
out to moonlight at a rural emergency room, which
I did once a month to make money so that we could
visit home at Christmas time. An hour into my tour

of duty, a fireman came in with chest pain. We hooked him up to the monitor and he had some irregular heart rhythms. "I'm going deaf now, doc. Is that normal?" he said. I reassured him and we turned on the defibrillator, which we used to shock the heart back to normal. "I'm going blind now, doc. Is that normal?" I once again reassured him, noting that he was still conscious. "I'm dying now," he said as his tracing went flat on the monitor in front of my eyes. I shocked him and he immediately woke up and looked at me and said, "Doc, you saved my life." All within the span of one day, one twenty-four hour period, from the depths of failure to the heights of success. Life is not always that dramatic, but in every person's life, on every day, there is a real possibility that failure may be followed by success, that despair may give way to hope and that faith may find its just reward.

# Be A Dreamer

*"If a man does not keep pace with his companions,*
*perhaps it is because he hears a different drummer.*
*But let him step to the music he hears,*
*however measured or far away."*

HENRY DAVID THOREAU

Trish and I were high school sweethearts. She's kept an eye on me since I was 15. So you might imagine she often knows what's going on in my head before I do. We were married and had our first child while I was in Medical School, expanded the family by two more during five years in surgical residency, and added a fourth as I began practice. Yet, within a few years of going out on my own, she could see that surgery alone would not sustain me. It was not what I dreamed about. One early morning, when the kids were still asleep and we sat there drinking coffee, she let me know it was all right to switch if I wanted. "Just find a way to get paid for it," she cautioned. So I spent some time planning out my options and finding a possible solution that might work. And it didn't work out exactly as I had planned, because that's the nature of things. But it worked out nonetheless. For planning and dreaming are two different things. Planning expects results while dreaming is its own reward. There's an old saying, "When man plans, God laughs at him, but when man dreams, God laughs with him."

# Preserve The Child

*"Every child is an artist. The problem is*
*how to remain an artist once he grows up."*

PABLO PICASSO

erhaps it is children's ability to openly experience love and instinctively react to it that sep-
arates them from adults encumbered by
weighty analysis. Perhaps it is their open faces, the
way they express joy, the way they come into your
life with a running skip and throw themselves trust-
ingly through the air believing you will catch them.
Children love who they are. Mike was a great talker
and storyteller. Mitch was an amazing creative force
and humorist. Marc kept us alive with constant
movement and planning. And Meredith, even though
the youngest, was always drawing her brothers into
play and instructing them simultaneously. So now
we have a poet, and a painter, and a sociologist and
an early childhood educator who still keeps a close
eye on those three boys. Our career counseling to
them: "Do something you're passionate about. And
do something that will leave this world just a little bit
better for your effort. But don't lose sight of who you
are." Some years ago, I was in a half-day strategic

planning session and bored to tears. I wrote on top of the pad, "A Few of My Favorite Things." One thing led to another, and soon I had 100 items. Eighty-seven of them were born in my childhood. Charles Kingley once said, "We act as though comfort and luxury were the chief requirements of life, when all that we need to make us really happy is something to be enthusiastic about."

# Find The Good In All

*"If heaven made him, earth can
find some use for him."*

CHINESE PROVERB

There is a little piece of redemption in even the most difficult or limited human being. Life is never perfectly good, nor perfectly bad, but always in between. My mother-in-law always says, "For every old sock, there's an old shoe." I found that easier to believe than to acknowledge the presence of redeeming grace in those who routinely abuse power. However, there is one phrase from The Lord's Prayer that I have found helpful for many years. It is "Forgive us our trespasses, as we forgive those who trespass against us." I find it helpful because when one begins by acknowledging one's own imperfections, it seems much easier to release anger or prejudice directed at another's shortcomings. I by no means have this one licked. Like driving too fast, I'll probably be working on it for the rest of my life. But searching for the good in everyone is an effort worth making because it is the doorway toward maximizing your own human potential.

# Be A Friend To Yourself

*"I desire to conduct the affairs of this administration, that if at the end... I have lost every friend on the earth, I shall have one friend left, and that friend shall be down inside me."*

ABRAHAM LINCOLN

When all is said and done, you have to live with yourself. You have to like who you are and what you do. You have to release anger and the desire to blame yourself or others. You have to rejoice in your gifts and acknowledge your weaknesses and failures. St. Frances de Sales said, "Have patience with all things, but chiefly have patience with yourself. Do not lose courage in considering your own imperfections, but instantly set about remedying them—every day begin the task anew." Where will that renewal come from? It's a serious question to ask yourself. I once had a discussion with a retired teacher who cautioned me about being out of balance. He noted that over the years every Friday night he would head to the university to write and return on Sunday morning. He said he had produced more than 100 published papers and that a couple of them were actually good. But he had found that his two daughters were now grown up, that they didn't know him and that they had no interest in being with him. Revitalization and renewal for the positive leader comes from investing time and presence in positive, hope-filled relationships. Being a friend to yourself means being a friend to your spouse and kids. Being a friend to yourself means being well rested. Being a friend to yourself means avoiding being consumed by greed or power or possessions. Mark Twain said, "A man cannot be comfortable without his own approval of his self."

# Postscript

NO MATTER HOW positive you are, you must confront uncertainty, for life and loss are interwoven. Positive leaders feel deeply and are as vulnerable as they are durable. Their responsiveness to crisis places them in great demand. Their ability to survive and thrive reflects a unique attitude toward loss. At their core, positive leaders are learners who seek out the lesson with each experience. They see the world as overflowing with opportunity for all and understand that delaying an opportunity in the interest of honoring more pressing obligations is not an opportunity forever lost. They have great faith and memory, which allows them to feel and experience the presence of loved ones even in their absence. Finally, they uniquely fill the voids in their lives, finding productive ways to contribute. The positive leader is at peace.

# Fill The Void

*"Where you used to be there is a hole in the world which I find myself constantly walking around in the daytime, and falling into at night. I miss you like hell."*
<br>
EDNA ST. VINCENT MILLAY

Ten years ago, my mother called me abruptly from Florida one day to let me know she was coming up to be checked. She had a sense that something was wrong. The following day, we found that she had widespread ovarian cancer. She underwent surgery and chemotherapy and did well for about a year, at which time she had a recurrence. Around the same time, our first child was married. The two events dramatically placed us in the middle of our lifeline. Here we sat with my mother rapidly approaching the final days of her life and our oldest son and his wife positioning themselves to create new life. Loss is inevitable. Loss of family or friends, loss of relationships and occasionally lost opportunities. What marks positive leaders is how they fill the void. It may be filled with positive memories and reminders that keep faith and hope alive, or equally with bitterness, anger and regret that widen the gap until it overtakes other living things. The loss may be viewed as a failure, or as an opportunity to bring success out of failure. When there is a loss, something is missing. When I was 12, our family sustained a terrible tragedy. My sister, Mary, who was four years old, drowned. It exposed our vulnerability and tested our relationships as blame and guilt bounced from one family member to the next. For 18 months we struggled with the absence and the pain. Then one spring morning, my youngest sister, Annbeth, was born—the embodiment of life and spirit and hope. Her birth signaled our survival. I noticed that my father began to whistle again. Twenty years later, when our own Meredith was born, I saw so much Annbeth in her, so much so that if I'm tired, I sometimes call her Annbeth by mistake. I recently had a birthday and was feeling kind of flat. When I got home from work, there was a present from Annbeth. She has a music degree and runs a music school for children. I opened the package and there was a tape. The card explained she had filled the tape with all types of music she thought I would like. I turned it on and the music filled the house. It lifted my spirit. The next morning, I found myself whistling her tunes. It is only those who lose dreaming, who are lost. A positive leader has the energy, the faith and the hope to fill the void in a manner that honors the loss.

# Be At Peace

*"There is room enough at the top for everyone."*

TRISH MAGEE

I was raised in an extremely competitive family. This provided me with energy and desire and a great deal of stamina. But what I found in my early years was that the goals that I set for myself became meaningless as soon as they were reached. This created a pattern of dissatisfaction and non-contentment. Beyond that there was an undercurrent of inability to share the joys of others' achievements, since, by definition, winning is about being at the top. And if someone else is there, you're not. About 10 years ago my wife, when she sensed this inappropriate behavior, began reminding me each time it occurred: "There is room enough at the top for everyone." Taken to heart, the thought is very profound. First, it means that your personal success does not need to be tied to someone else's failure. Secondly, it reinforces the belief that supporting others and their successes can be incorporated into your own view of success. Finally, it preaches patience; for if there is truly enough room at the top for everyone, you need not seize every opportunity that arises for fear that that opportunity will be forever lost. That extra room at the top means that there is room for you as well as everyone else. The opportunities will appear again. One priority may be displaced by another for a period of time without completely abandoning the vision no matter how strong. And if one can be patient, and supportive and capable of rejoicing in another's success, then peace will follow. Because each changed life signals renewed hope as one life touches another, and then another, and society begins to reflect the difference. Because, after all, "civilization is just a slow process of learning to be kind."

# A Final Note

Time carries with it change. Nine years have passed since the first edition of this book. Much has changed. In the moments of joy, we all rejoiced. In the moments of sadness, we have grieved, but also discovered a surprising strength and resilience. Each challenge brings forth new heroes, like my sister Sue. She spoke the words we all felt on the day of our father's burial. They are repeated on the following pages and capture perfectly the love we enjoyed from and between our parents.

*O*ne time before Mom and Dad were sick with their dreadful diseases I was visiting Steve and we were talking about heroes. Steve said his hero was Dad. I asked him why. He said, "Think about it. Dad went to work every day, was out of the house early and went till late in the evening, often got called to the hospital in the middle of the night and always made rounds on the weekend...but, never complained. You never heard Daddy complain about how hard he worked."

Dad was a man of compassion. We were all frustrated at times when we would come home from school with a story about some annoying little classmate and Dad would feel compelled to insist that we think about what that child might be living with that would make him react the way he had. Dad always thought of the other side of an issue. When I was younger I thought he did it just to tease me (he was a masterful teaser after all) but as I got older, and, certainly now, I am convinced it was because that is how he saw the world and the people in it. And, it was his compas-

*sion that helped people, and healed those who were losing their spirit for life.*

*All of us, while we were growing up, were stopped by people in Fort Lee who felt compelled to tell us how wonderful our father was. For me, at the time, it was an uncomfortable situation—I didn't know them and they would be pinching my cheek and filled with emotion would say, "Your father is a great doctor and a great man." Today I would have to say I agree—He certainly was.*

*He was hard working. He was a man with heart. He was a gentleman. He was a busy man who did not ask much for himself. His pleasure and the only thing he really seemed to need in life was Mom. And we all knew it. His busy life, the responsibility of raising 12 children and his love for Mom meant that none of us have memories of Dad dawdling away a day with us alone, but what we do have, straight to our very core, is what it means to be devoted to someone and what it means to love someone—and we know that because of Dad and Mom. We know that when you love someone you give everything you have, and you don't measure how much you've given, and you don't measure how much you receive. Although Dad didn't spend a lot of individual time with us, he shaped our world quietly and powerfully.*

*Dad loved Mom heart and soul and his love brought out*

*the best in her. And we, through the grace of God, were blessed to be a part of what came from that love. Every day he went to work to earn the money it took to keep a roof over our heads and our bodies fed. The example he set encouraged education and high aspirations. He foot the bill for many of us to attend private high schools and all of us to continue on to college. He taught us honesty. I was a little girl when Dad first impressed upon me the importance of honesty. He related a story to me about his own childhood. He had gone to the store and when he paid the shopkeeper there was some question about the amount of change he was due. He said more, the shopkeeper was uncertain but took Dad's word because he said, "He had never known Bill Magee to tell a lie." He finished that story by saying to me, "There is nothing more important than honesty. People may not always like what you have to say, but if they can believe you then they will always trust you." That was a lesson Dad taught over and over again. His personal honesty and his integrity were beyond reproach.*

*Dad's final lesson for me was one that taught bravery and humility, again through his example. When Dad was diagnosed with Alzheimer's Disease, Mom already had cancer. Throughout the years to come I do not remember Dad talking about his disease. He must have been worried about what the future would hold. He must have been frustrated by his loss of ability. Long before he reached the stage of being unaware of his surroundings …Long before*

*Alzheimer's robbed him of his memories and his abilities completely, he was losing small things. He lost the ability to drive. He lost the ability to read. He couldn't remember his children's faces. He couldn't participate in conversations appropriately. He couldn't follow conversations. He couldn't tell time. He didn't recognize his friends. He couldn't order food in a restaurant because he couldn't remember what different types of food were called. He needed help in the bathroom. He couldn't remember how to tie his shoes...All this, yet he was still aware enough to know that this was happening to him. And through it all, Dad talked about Mom, her care, her treatment and about other things in life.*

*Dad was a brave man and with every personal loss he suffered he did it silently. He did it humbly. He did it with a firm faith in God and that faith shaped his life and gave him the strength to live it so well.*

*"This too will pass honey," it was a favorite saying of Dad's, and it often came with a gentle smile. And so it has. Gone is the wonderful time when Mom and Dad were alive and healthy and filled with a love for life...when you could wrap your arms around them and feel their warm embrace.*

*Dad is now with Mom and there is a great comfort in that. And he lives on in us: His children, grandchildren and great-grandchildren and there is wonderful joy in that. But, I know that I am not alone when I say that I loved him dearly and will miss him terribly.*

*May God bless all of us as we close this chapter of our lives and may God bless Daddy as he begins his new life in heaven.*

Eulogy by Sue Magee Ross for William P. Magee, MD
September 21, 1998

Mom and Dad's values live on in their children and grandchildren.

# About the Author

Mike Magee, MD directs the Pfizer Medical Humanities Initiative and is editor of HealthPolitics.com. A Senior Fellow in Humanities at the World Medical Association and an Honorary Master Scholar at the New York University School of Medicine, Dr. Magee has been termed by the Boston Globe "The most optimistic physician in America."